The Small Business Guide To Success

Book 1

Written By Anthony S. Owens

Chapters:

1. Life Before The Plunge
2. Education Isn't Always A College Degree
3. What No One Ever Tells You
4. To Be Or Not To Be
5. Procrastination Is A Strategy
6. Failure Is Always An Option
7. Yelp Is Your Enemy
8. The City Always Wants A Cut

Dedication:
This book is dedicated to all of your success.

Anthony Owens

May you have the hindsight to know where you've been, the foresight to know where you are going, and the insight to know when you have gone too far.

A Note From The Author:

Sometimes in life an opportunity arises. Whether it be the chance at a career change, a move to a new city or even something as small as saving a few dollars on something because you were in the right place at the right time. Some people will see the chance and jump on it, and some people will follow the routine they already have and never aspire to do anything else.

When starting your own business is the focus of change, its considered entrepreneurship. The propose of this book is to provide the average person whom wants to start a business a step by step guide to their dream. This book is for the people that would rather struggle for the short term just to make their

dream become a reality. This book is for the people that realize the skill or service they provide is essential to the world around them and outline a path to get them to the people needing it.
This is not your average marketing book. This book will tell you the good, the bad, the ugly, and the unspoken.

This book will outline steps that many of my clients have followed and made themselves into formidable competition in their respective fields.
I hope you enjoy and I hope that this book allows you to understand the inner workings of the small business world..

Thanks for reading.

Chapter 1
Life Before The Plunge

So, you are sitting in your cubicle, staring at the same beat up bulletin board and wired handset telephone, day in and day out. Wondering how your going to be able to not come back to this job after lunch and still make a living. Depending on how you want to approach this, you have 2 different options.

Your first option of is to come back after lunch and talk your now unhangry self out of throwing your little trash can across the office and screaming "Sianara" to Jim from accounting as you storm past his office on your way out of the building. Then come in on time faithfully for the next 20 years just to get laid off 3 weeks from retirement.

With this option you really don't have to do anything at all.

You just continue being the person who never took the chance to be great. You never took the chance to see where your potential could take you. You were the kind of person too scared to let go of the security of a meager pay check in search of your fortune. If see yourself as someone option one applies to, then this book probably isn't for you.

The second option isn't really an option. Its more like a state of mind. The second option is entrepreneurship. If your reading this then you probably already have a pretty good idea of what I'm talking about and where I'm going to take you in this book.

Some people have the drive and determination to think of something and figure out a way to market it and sell it for a profit. Some people start this young by selling candy or trading cards, Hell some people retire and decide to finally launch their business. The beauty of option 2 is it doesn't matter how long it takes you to realize its the best option, as long as your still alive you can choose it..

Your second option is to figure out what in your life have you done, that you have enough experience in to sell and make a living.

Ask yourself a few key questions.

Do you like crafts, cutting hair, graphic design, or cooking?

Do you have enough experience in your thing to make it a thing people want?

Do you know a guy willing to pay for one thing you can get from another guy cheaper and turn around and make a buck selling it to the first guy? Can you broker a deal between 2 businesses and make a residual commission from one or both of the parties involved?

If you said yes to any of the questions above, you probably have what it takes to start your own business

The list of things someone could possibly do as a successful business is literally infinite. There is something that almost any person with more than 3 brain sells can do for themselves to make a living.

Do you have a lawn mower and a weed eater in your garage you only use 2 or 3 times a month? Well you already have the main ingredients to a landscaping company. Do you have a Cricut or Cameo craft cutter? The custom card and decal industries are booming.

Do you have a 599 piece tool set you got from Harbor Freight to change a part on your car and now they are just collecting dust? Sounds to me like a light mechanical repair service is sitting on your shelf.

Do you have Adobe Photo shop and a decent camera or drone?

Seems like you may have a startup photography studio or overhead shot production company on your hands.

Do you have a van or truck and a strong back?
Can somebody say " Moving Company"

With the internet being a trove of useful information, You could become an expert on something in a few short weeks and start your business from there. All you have to do is educate yourself and make a decision to want more than a 9 to 5 has to offer.

Don't start your business with the delusion that within the next year your going to be buying private jets and mega yachts.

If that is your goal you better have something really good to begin with and 1 heck of a marketing team. It can and has been done but this book is for your average Joe wanting to start a small business, not ole' Donny boy starting out with a small loan of 5 million dollars from daddy.

Life before the plunge may be monotonous and boring. But life after the plunge can be exactly the same. It could also be the most exciting and rewarding thing you will ever do. So weigh your options wisely and pick one. If you want it bad enough the pages that follow will explain exactly how to do it.

Chapter 2
<u>Education Isn't Always A College Course</u>

Ever heard the old saying "Fake It Until You Make It"?

Just that saying may have some of you thinking,
I'm about to tell you to engage in some college bribing racket or to get yourself a fake degree from a degree mill named The University of South Eastern Dumbledore Tech.
But I'm Not.

In some cases your new business idea may require the consultation of local and regional city zoning and ordinance boards and or may be required to have some kind of licensing or certification to start up and operate for a profit. In those cases, college may be the only education you can acquire to preform those services.

For the average Joe wanting to start a business, most of the time your not trying to start a pharmaceutical lab or highly regulated manufacturing company or any other super special- ized, highly regulated company. Most of the time you are going to want to start an accounting firm or a bakery, a mechanic shop or food truck, a landscaping company or a doggy day care.

No matter what you want to do, the inter- net can provide you some kind of tutorial. I remember when I started my residential and commercial lint removal company, My first way to push it was letting a lady from Yelp talk me into starting a Pro Page or what ever they call it. She gave me $300 dollars worth of free yelp ads as an incentive to try out their platform.

I really didn't understand the process but I agreed just to see how it went.

I won't go too deep into this story as I have dedicate a whole chapter later in the book as to why Yelp and other sites like Yelp are literally the scourge of the online marketing and advertisement industry.

The reason I tell that story, stop and then refer back to it is, When I was using Yelp I was getting business almost instantly.

Unfortunately my account manager at Yelp was not quite paying attention to what I said my businesses primary service was. Instead of posting my business as Dryer Lint Removal Service she posted me as an Appliance Repair Service.

Mind you, being new to Yelp I had no idea that she had directed a whole different type of client to me.

My service was supposed to be cleaning out dryer exhaust systems however all my messages for service were for appliance repair.

My first service request was from someone needing their dishwasher looked at.. It was a request from a giant insurance company. They said it wasn't draining and was leaving spots on all the glasses.

I sat in front of my computer looking at the request and trying to decide how these people possibly figured since I offered dryer exhaust cleaning it qualified me to fix their dishwasher.

After a minuet or two of pondering a thought snapped into my head.

I have Insurance that allows me to do handyman work I don't see how this could be considered anything other than just that. So with that in mind I quickly tried to figure out how I could fix this dishwasher with no prior experience. I messaged the client back and said I would be glad to come out and take a look, but I was booked solid until tomorrow morning.. The client responded that would be fine and scheduled a time for the next day. Once the appointment was set, I asked for the model number and brand of the dishwasher. They replied with the model number and brand of the dishwasher and also asked what the diagnosis fee would be.

This is where "Fake it Until You Make It" comes into play.

For dishwasher repair I don't think anyone was in danger of me trying to fix this thing and make a buck.

However, I had no idea what someone would charge to fix a dishwasher much less how much they would charge to diagnose what was wrong with it. I instantly began searching for a company's phone number I had heard about on the radio. I figured If they were paying for 10 ads a day on I heart radio and had a fleet of 35 trucks running in all of the cities around me, they were probably charging the most to come out and look at a problem and fix it.

I found the number and called them. I told them what dishwasher "I" had and what my problem was. I asked how long it would be before they could send someone out. They said 48 hours out was their soonest appointment. I then asked what their diagnostic fee was. They said $75 dollars. Then I said " do you run into this problem a lot with this model?"

Their response was that, that particular model was plagued with problems. I asked if they had a ball park what it could cost me to get it fixed and they said no more than $400 with the labor and parts included.

I said thank you and that I wanted to shop the ballpark around and that I would call back later.

Wallah

Now I know how much it will cost to have the best and most expensive company come out to do the work. Now I had to respond to my clients question about the diagnostic fee. I answered the message with a price of $65. However I said that if they decided to have me fix the issue that $65 would go towards the final total of the bill and not be a separate fee.. They responded that my fee was satisfactory and said they would see me less than 24 hours later..

But wait, I had to be there and fix this thing. I didn't know the first thing about dishwashers. Aside from the fact that if you didn't wash your plate off before you put it in, it would clog up the drain and cause your wife to say mean things to you..

What was I going to do?

Its not hard to figure out what I did if your reading this book. You probably saw my solution coming from the very beginning of this story.

But for those of you that are reading and don't know what my solution was, I'll tell you. And its two separate words

GOOGLE + YOUTUBE

I took the information I had been given, which was merely the brand and model number and looked up the problem description on google.

whirlpool+the model number+won't drain leaving spots on glassware

Instantly my screen was populated with thousands of search results most relevant to my keywords..
At the top of the page were videos of what I should do and then below them was infinite links to forums with people experiencing the same problems.

You wouldn't believe the absolute plethora of information I was able to obtain in less than 1 hour reading and watching videos about this particular issue with this particular dishwasher. The main conclusion people came to in these forums was that the filter being clogged was the reason for not draining and an excess build up of Final rinse solution would leave spots on the glassware. Just like that I was quite confident I would be able to look at this thing and determine what it needed. But being a totally different type of cleaning company I didn't have the supplies or tools on hand I would need to actually fix the issue.

The next morning 2 hours before I was supposed to be at the appointment I knew I needed some things to preform a really detailed cleaning of this appliance. I went to the closest dollar store and started to pick up things I would need.

I bought a small bucket, some cleaning sponges and rags, a bottle of orange clean, a package of long pipe cleaners, a turkey baster, and a small multi tipped screw driver. I spend less than $10 dollars and now I had everything I thought I could possibly need to do this job..

I got to the appointment about 35 minuets early and again watched a few of the most relevant videos I found the day before..

I left the tools in the truck and went in to meet with the company liaison. I looked at the dishwasher and noticed all the issues mentioned in the forums. I then told the liaison that I would need to unclog the drain and clean the filter and clean the excess spot remover that had hardened in the dispenser out. I told her if she was satisfied with the diagnosis and wanted me to continue the cost would be $320 dollars.

She was very happy with the price and told me to proceed.

At that moment I was officially a dishwasher repair man for the day. I completed the task by literally spending 1 hour thoroughly cleaning the inside of this thing.

After I was done she handed me a check and thanked me for my service. I got in the elevator with my $10 dollars worth of supplies and my $320 dollar check and rejoiced as the

task was done and the money was in the bank.. The next day she called me back. I saw the number on my caller ID and thought great, time to refund the money its back on the fritz. I answered. After the pre conversation pleasantries, I asked how it was working.

She proceeded to tell me how amazed she was at how clean the glassware was and that everyone

extremely happy with the service that I had provided. She wanted to add me to their permanent vendor list.

This chapter is about not necessarily

needing college or specialized training to get something done. Sometimes its just a matter of asking the right questions in the right places and being confident in yourself that you can execute the task as it was explained in a video or forum. Quite literally any question you have about any task has a place on today's internet. With a few clicks and a few keywords you too can conquer unfamiliar tasks for cash..

Remember
"Faking It Until You Make It"
Isn't always unacceptable. With 2 hours and $10 you can make $320 dollars by just going a little way out of your lane.

Chapter 3
<u>What No One Ever Tells You</u>

Well by definition this chapter will tell you the things no one else has had the insight or time to go over with you.
Its about the unspoken tricks some people use to get ahead.
The subtle nuances that go into closing every deal they do.

Its about what every smart business owner has to take into account for when doing any kind of planning or execution of said plan. There will be a few phrases that will be the corner stones of this chapter.

The First and most important to me is "Adapt and Overcome"

Well what does that mean you ask. It means that no matter what happens you have to be able to adjust your plan. The good the bad and the ugly can and will happen at anytime without any warning. In order to become successful you will need to be able to do this in its most basic form. You can't let a sudden expense or setback throw off the entire plan.

Always have a what if fund. If don't have whats needed to have that fund there are always other options.

Some times a plan can go so well that you can't handle the influx of work that has fallen into your lap. This is where my second most important saying comes into play.

" I would rather have more work than I can handle, than not enough work to survive"

There is always a way to get the work done. Even if your a one man or woman band somebody somewhere can help you accomplish your work. You can rely on the freelance network like Fiverr.com or Upwork.com and get access to thousands of freelance workers. They quite literally have everything you would need in any situation.

Staffing solution companies can help in a pinch as well. They give you access to the local work force at a set price. You pay them as 1099 subcontractors and they pay the workers. It cuts out your need for insurance, tax deduction and pay roll services.

You could even goes as far as joining a Facebook group in your area that specializes in job listings from local businesses. You would be surprised how many unemployed and freelance workers monitor these groups for quick and inconsistent work.

This brings us to the my third favorite saying
" You can never grow to fast"

Growth of your business should never been seen as a bad thing. Growing too fast and not knowing how to handle the growth is. That is probably the reason this book is so important to the reader. I'm telling you from years of experience working in multiple industries, If you grow and don't know how to keep up the growth can kill your business.

Not only can it kill your business and business relationships some times it carries over into your personal life.

One person trying to do the work of 4

people is sometimes something you can do. But in most cases the overall service and all related relationships are adversely affected by the operators inability to adapt to the growth.

You can't start a business and not expect it to grow beyond what you can handle. If you are working 80 hours a week and sleeping at the office just to get through all the emails and billing so you can start service early the next day, You should probably think about finding some help.

You can justify it easily if you meet the last description. You are quite literally shooting yourself in the foot and trying to walk to the store. You will never get anywhere with all the weight of that business on your shoulders and a wound in your foot.

My fourth favorite saying is

"One Small Flee Can Drive A Big Dog Crazy"

This means exactly what you think it does. Or maybe it doesn't. It means quite frankly that even if your starting out and don't have any momentum you can still be competition to the other guy.

Something as simple as a landing page or a simple social media account can put you in front of the same customers that the big dog has been in front of for some time. Just that alone will bring you untold amounts of business. Every industry has the Big Dog in the area. Whether its the largest towing company or the largest graphics company in the area, you can rest assured that not everyone they helped was satisfied with the service they received and are looking for a new provider.

Just having a Facebook page with useful information can bring those clients to you instead of the Big Dog. Remember just starting out everyone is a Big Dog to you. So the supply of customers will be there, all you have to do is be visible.

The last saying Ill leave you with in this title is
"Karma is a B****"

I need not got to deep into explaining this premise.

It is exactly how it sounds.

No matter what you do in life the winds of Karma are at your back, just waiting for the right time to switch and put you on your backside...

If you step on toes or do something shifty on your rise to the top Karma will always remember. She works in mysterious ways. You may think your even but only she has the control. My best practice is not to step on toes at all.. If you have to, make sure you are putting back just as much positive effort and try to soften the blow. I have learned for experience, your actions always have an equal and opposite reaction. And sometimes Karma can put you in a rock bottom situation.

I lied, I'm going to go way back into my history with this saying, but everyone has heard it one way or another. "Don't Get To Big For Your Britches"

Meaning, know your role. Don't go to far trying to look cool or make a point. Stay Humble. Well at least until you have 10 million, I think that is the safe number where you could retire to some desert Island and be as un-person-able as you would like.

Just take these few sayings to heart. These alone are my building blocks to a successful you and a thriving business.

Chapter 4
To Be Or Not To BE

You may think that I'm about to go off on some Shakespearean philosophical tangent, but I digress.
This chapter is about the question every small business owner struggles with right before they take the plunge. To be or not to be, its really one hell of a question.

You are past the point of the thought of entrepreneurship, but not quite to the point of quitting the ole 9 to 5 and the securities it comes along with. Trying to decide whether you have the idea and the skills that will pay the bills. Asking yourself questions like who would want what I offer, how do I get my information to them, or I wonder what I should charge.

Like I said before some of you reading this already know how to get into the field your after. But for others just wanting a way out of the monotony the 9 to 5 life offers, it can be much more difficult to get started.

Ask your self the questions:

What skills or services can I provide?

Do you have a hidden talent or hobby you could exploit to gain revenue? Can you draw, do you have a great speaking voice, can you sing or write content?

Do you know how to fix R/C cars or computers? The list of things is staggering. I'm quite positive that if you really put you mind to it you could come up with something to start your business.

Now that you have decided what you can do ask yourself this.

How many others are doing this as a business?

Get on google or Bing and research the competition.

Lets say you live in a big city and you want to do Vinyl Vehicle Lettering. You would want to find out how many other competitors are in your market. Sometimes an over saturated market can mean an extreme need for the service you provide or that the market is full and you will literally starve while picking up their crumbs. One upside to this situation is that you are in a position to take the clients that they lost due to any number of factors.

In a super saturated market you will have to make sure your business is as visible as possible. Google listings and other forms of advertising will be necessary to drive the lost clients in your direction. Big city living always costs more, and in return the price to compete in its markets are also a little more pricey.

If you live in a more scenic area, you are less likely to have such stiff competition. Unless you are doing something that lots of other folks in your small area is doing. In small towns and townships internet marketing isn't as important as word of mouth. Anybody that lives or lived in a small town knows how they talk. The best kind of publicity in these areas is always going to be word of mouth.

You will need to do more public events or sponsor more local little league type teams to really get your name circulating in the community. But once its moving you can rest assured your business will see the gains. You can also attend the local church and volunteer your time there for certain functions and that too will drive positive attention towards you and your business.

If you know you can do it, but are just scared to take the chance, remember this, Scared Money Doesn't Make Money. If it doesn't make dollars, then it doesn't make sense. If you have a marketable and in demand business idea when your through asking yourself the questions above, then do it.

The answer is, To Be is better than to Not.

Chapter 5
<u>Procrastination is a Strategy</u>

This chapter by far is my favorite to write. This chapter is going to go over the ways not just jumping right into something can be beneficial. Technically in most cases its the illusion of procrastination. Most of the time when this is your strategy you have already done what need to be done, you just haven't presented it to the world yet.

Lets take for example when I do something for a client. Sometimes you get the work done so fast you don't want the client to question the price.

Well why did I pay $65 dollars for something that took you 10 minuets to do. The easy answer is your paying for my experience and service. Its not my fault Fred took 3 hours for the same $65 dollar task. Both of us may have provided the same service but mine was done just as well or better in less time.

But in some cases you need to be able to stretch the perception of how long you took to complete the task.
For example Some web designer take weeks or months to turn out a fully functioning E- commerce website. They tell you that its coming along and keep the service going as long as they can to pick every dime they can from your pocket. Most of the time your

website was done the first week and they drug out the process to make you think you were paying for all of this time and effort from their team.

The reality is they used procrastination as a strategy.

Another form of procrastination as a strategy comes from the credit card industry. This may go against everything you have ever thought but I read a book called Rich Dad, Poor Dad a long time ago.

The one thing I took from the book was really relevant to my situation at the time. The general meaning of the term to be short was Pay Yourself First.

Lets say you have a Credit Card bill that you struggle every month to pay off. Did you know that paying the minimum payment doesn't adversely affect your credit score. Most people actually keep a balance so that they can maintain the credit scores they have. Why pay a huge chunk every month. Adopt the minimum payment for the first few months and save the rest.

Then after 4 months of payments you can call your card company and ask if they would take a smaller lump some to close out the payment owed. Most times they will do this.. Immediately use your card again to keep the account open and follow the same steps. Your credit only gets better and you end up saving money on the interest.

There are literally hundreds of ways procrastination can make or save you money. Lets say that you have a situation where two separate entities want to purchase your product exclusively.

Both companies are offering you

the same price and terms for the purchase. But you want more for what you have to offer.

The easiest is to counter offer somewhere in a range you know they would be willing to pay.

(This is an important part of the process. Don't be greedy because what I'm about to tell you to do requires the right amount of finesse, the right price, and the perfect amount of procrastination. Anything outside the lines will pretty much railroad your negotiation)

Once you put your final offer on the table, go dark.

Don't answer phone calls or texts or emails for no less than 18 hrs. This alone will put a sense of urgency in the minds of your investors.

Some people will tell you that what I'm saying in this book is leading you the wrong way. But trust me when I tell you these things. I have seen this negotiation technique work more times than I can count. And in almost every case the risk was low and the reward was high.

After your 18 hour sabbatical from communications, 1 or both of your negotiation partners will have worried their deal would fall through and made necessary arrangements to accommodate your offer. One may have already agreed. Then again for larger negotiations the 18 hr window may be 14 days. In each situation the time can be adjusted to make it look as if your not desperate to close the deal. Desperation will cost you money when closing.

You can apply this strategy as you see fit in your business. It will definitely make a difference once your prefect the technique.

There are a few more sayings I would like to bestow on you.
I would like to break them down here as they pertain to procrastination being a very viable strategy.

John F Kennedy once said "We must use time as a tool, not as a crutch. "

Knowing when to procrastinate can be a priceless skill.

Another is " Don't put off until tomorrow what you can do today"

This is true most of the time. Unless you finished it today and want to make it look as if it took until tomorrow to complete.

The next one is " Better 3 hours too soon than 1 minuet too late"

Finish the work early but present it right on time. Don't make what your doing look to easy for the price you gave.. Wanting to complete a task quickly is great but don't sell yourself short on future en devours.

Don't be fooled by the calendar. There are only as many days in the year as you make use of. One man gets only a week's value out of a year while another man gets a full year's value out of a week.

Its the same when providing your service. Remember the perception of time can always be manipulated to add a perceived value to your service. And perception is everything.

Don't be afraid to make it look like it took longer than it did.

Chapter 6
<u>Failure Is Always An Option</u>

Time to get to the scariest issue plaguing today's entrepreneurs. Failure
The other F word that offends everyone. Failure can be seen as defeat more times than it can be considered a blessing. But in some cases failure is not only a option , it could be your only option to save your otherwise sickly business.

In the case of a small retail shop, you may be faced with a decline in income due to any number of circumstances in the world around you.

You may find yourself struggling to find funding or struggling to pay for your next order of inventory.

Sometimes the answer is as easy as a going out of business sale. There are several large retailers who have ran going out of business sales since they opened their doors. Just the words going out of business trigger something in a lot of people that compels them into browsing your inventory.

Having a sale like this at a strategic time, could likely be the answer to all of your prayers. If you didn't want to do it at your main location to avoid confusion, you could get a banner made and take your inventory to a local flea market on the weekend. Kind of like an un-branded Going Out Of Business sale.

Just because you have an established location, does not mean going to a booth at a flee market is below you. Its actually a great way to put your brand in front of willing people with disposable income. If you fail because you didn't try that is one thing.

But if your failure is merely an illusion to bolster sales and exposure then it is totally acceptable and a very viable option.

Winston Churchill once said "Success is stumbling from failure to failure with no loss of enthusiasm."

Failure should never be seen as a discouraging encounter. It merely allows one to learn and grow. You can count on only 3 things in life, Death, Taxes, And Change.

Change is actually the only thing in life that stays exactly the same. Kind of ironic huh? The ability to actually deal and process with a true failure sets you apart from everyone else you will ever meet.

One time in my life I let a failure define who I was for almost a year. That one failure made me feel like I was less of a person. It literally ripped me to my core. It took me to a whole new level of low. I let that one failure define me. It took me almost a full year to pull myself back from that hole. The smartest and easiest way to get yourself

out of a hole is to quit digging down. That saying resonates with me to this day. It isn't because someone told me what I was doing was the worst thing I could possibly be doing. It was me reflecting back on where I went wrong. I had to stop blaming myself and actually start thinking about the true reason I had failed.

I was blaming me, instead of actually blaming the root of failure its self.

I had to address the miscommunications, late work, over whelming work load, supply issues, and becoming to big for my britches.

I of course played a huge roll in the failure because I didn't know how to maintain at the speed I was being required to go. I was so afraid to ask for help. I wanted so bad not to fail that it ended up being the only option I had..

And let me tell you, that is a feeling that is harder to shake than the failure it's self. Eventually I was able to learn from that fail and come out on top. It took 1 or 2 more but after overcoming the first failure I was able to deal with them in a timely manner and actually never lose a moment of work time in between.

Just remember,
You build on failure. You use it as a stepping stone. Close the door on the past. You don't try to forget the mistakes, but you don't dwell on it. You don't let it have any of your energy, or any of your time, or any of your space.

However, Failure is so important. We speak about success all the time. It is the ability to resist failure or use failure that often leads to greater success. I've met people who don't want to try for fear of failing. That in it's self is the ultimate and most unacceptable failure of all.

Failure is not the opposite of success , it's part of success. Don't bury your failures, let them inspire you. Failure defeats losers but it inspires winners. Failures are part of life. If you don't fail, you don't learn. If you don't learn you'll never change. Don't fear failure. Fear being in the exact same place next year as you are today. In order to succeed, you must

be willing to experience failure,
It's as simple as that.

Chapter 7
<u>Yelp Is Your Enemy</u>

Some of you will swear by Yelp and other services like Yelp, But to a grassroots marketeer those services are a scam. Sure they put you in front of people because they spend a ton on advertising, But they can do that because they extort the hard earned money from small business owners like yourself.

"Extort" How could you say that, you ask. First thing that Yelp does is add your business to its list of people to screw. By that I mean, even though you don't know what yelp is, your business is listed there. That doesn't sound like a bad thing until you realize you can't respond to reviews unless your a paid member. You literally have no control over the listing at all unless you are a paid member.

In my experience with them I jumped in feet first. I tend to not be one to follow trends, but in this case I thought it would help bolster my business. Even though I knew how to do everything they do I thought that I would just let them handle it. At first it was OK. OK is a loose term, because although they offered me the moon, and provided a ride half way there, they ended up dropping a meteor on my bank account.

More like an F bomb. I was roped in with the promise of a free trial. I was thinking like every smart business owner, if they are going to give me something for free, then I'll give it a try.

I initially didn't want to purchase anything, but the super convincing lady on the other end of the phone assured me that they could do wonders for my business. I had branched out from what I normally did and was trying to put myself at the top of an emerging market. I would have never entertained the idea of using a service like Yelp for my existing business, but for my start up I figured I'd give it a try.. The lady on the phone assured me that I would receive $300 in ads on yelp and that if I weren't happy with the service I wouldn't be charged.

Well I did it. I went for the free trial on the Yelp Premium Package that If I didn't cancel in thirty days would be charged the $150 a month. So I set up my Premium account with the lady on the phone. We went through every aspect of my business. Who my target market was, what my service was, and how I wanted to be seen. I uploaded my logos and info to my page and wallah. I now had "control" of my Yelp profile.

Mind you they had a page for my main business not my start up.

While on the phone with the lady from Yelp, she setup the marketing aspect of the page . She guaranteed me that I would see immediate business. I was stoked when we got off the phone. All I had was the tools and the know how to do the work. Now I felt like I was going to make it off the ground. I poked and prodded the page for the rest of the day learning how to utilize the software. That night I went to bed anticipating the new influx of business.

Late the next afternoon My phone dinged. To my delight a new client had found me on Yelp. I was so excited. Unfortunately the client was looking for someone to fix their dishwasher. My business focused on cleaning out the exhaust systems for dryers. However I had insurance that covered this type of work so my fake it till you make it approach was the only option. I asked her what the problem was and then I asked for an exact model number of her dishwasher.

I then made an appointment to come out and diagnose the problem the next day. I informed her about my $75 diagnostic fee and agreed. Some may ask how I could charge a diagnostic fee when I didn't know what I was doing. Well that answer is easy.

I knew that in order to get this job done and to get it done right, I would need to research. I spent the next 4 hours combing the inter-web trying to absorb all the knowledge that one could about this particular model of dishwasher. I looked though forums and group chats. I looked up schematics and asked google any and all possible ways to fix the issue. At the end of my search I felt pretty confident I could fix the issue.

The next day I got up early and refreshed my knowledge. I preformed to the best of my ability with what I knew. I took the entire thing apart and cleaned and rebuilt it in about 55 minuets.

I collected my check and went about my way. Sure Yelp provided me business but it was not for the service I was advertising for. The very next day another call about a dishwasher. Again I followed the same research steps and completed the task.

The next day I called my vendor at Yelp and expressed my concern.. Long story short I decided to cancel service. To my surprise at the end of that

month my card was charged $150. I had literally on recorded phone call been told my service would be canceled and I would not be charged. I disputed the charge and was refunded. I was assured by my bank it wouldn't happen again. So

30 days goes by again and what do you know another $150 dollar charge.

Again I dispute this and get my money back. This is all after canceling my free trial more than 10 days before the deadline. After all the communication with Yelp and begging them to stop over drafting my account I receive a collection letter.

To this day, Yelp is still trying to collect monthly payments from my old account. After the third month of them charging my bank account I finally left that bank and started a new account elsewhere. Not sure if they are still charging the account but Its no longer a problem. Ill wait until it hits my credit and dispute it with my evidence.

Yelp is not here to help you. It is here to force you into paying for something you don't need. With the right amount advertising budget and a few YouTube videos you can unlock the same doors they already know how to unlock for you.

The only ads and services I use are Facebook,Instagram,Twitter, and Google. If you too base these 4 platforms at the core of your advertising, you will see all the results you can get from Yelp without the headache of Yelp.

Chapter 8
The City Always Wants A Cut

This is something that the most savvy business owners will tell you. No matter what city or town it is they have figured out a way to make you pay to do business in their city limits. They even have citizens they pay to report you for running a business within the city. First things first, The United States Supreme Court ruled that towns and municipalities charging business owners a business licensing fee was unconstitutional.

Therefore cites and towns now charge

you a permitting fee through their respected (or unrespected) zoning departments. It's a complete ruse on the business owner but no one really wants to fight the city. Anyone who does fight usually gets a concession from the city, but not before spending untold amount of capital fighting the issue.

That leaves the small business under prepared. Sometimes cities put misleading information on their website in hopes you will mess up and then along with their tax they can levy a fine on you or your business as well. Unless your business directly monetarily benefits the city, they will try to fine or tax you for every dollar you don't fight to give them.

Not every city or town is like this, but at a certain point in their growth, they will all become money hungry and not care who's pocket their taxes come from.

This is the shortest chapter in this book.

I only wrote this to give you a heads up. ALWAYS make sure you know what cut your going to give to the city, so they get it first. If they don't get it first they always have a way and a statute to get more.

Stay tuned for our next installment which will cover taxes, budget marketing, the barter system and more.
Thanks for reading and we look forward to helping you and your business succeed.

NOTES:

Anthony Owens

Anthony Owens

The Small Business Guide to Success : Book 1

Anthony Owens

Anthony Owens

www.ingramcontent.com/pod-product-compliance
Lightning Source LLC
Chambersburg PA
CBHW021904170526
45157CB00005B/1960